Maintaining and Operating Your Computer

RON GREENER

Table of Contents

Introduction

This text consists of a wide assortment of procedures that can be done on your computer in order to keep it performing well. It is intended for the home computer. The maintenance of an office or business computer is best left to the responsible tech department.

The book was originally designed using the Windows XP operating system. It has since been modified for Windows Vista and Windows 7.

All of the procedures have been tried thoroughly and repeatedly and should offer no harm to your computer. However, it is strongly advised that you backup your My Documents, Desktop, and Favorites folders prior to making any changes.

Parts of a Computer

Clock (2 GHz)

Controls speed of microprocessor. Advertised: 2GHz (2,000,000,000 instructions per second)

Hard Disk

Purpose: Permanent storage for programs and data files, that is, Windows, Word, Excel, Internet Explorer, pictures, songs, letters, reports, etc
Advertised: 500GB
500GB= 500,000,000,000 Byte locations

Display

Gets bytes from memory for creating screen images

Microprocessor

Central piece of hardware.
4 billion transistors
Purpose: execute program instructions
Advertised: Pentium or AMD

Memory

RAM (Random Access Memory)
Purpose: Temporary Storage for Programs and data files. Programs must be transferred from the Hard Disk into memory in order to run
Advertised: 2GB (2,000,000,000) byte locations)
Very important to have at least 2GB for good performance

Key-board

Typing sends bytes to memory

Modem

Converts bytes from memory into analog signals for communicating to the Internet

Mouse

Sends signals to memory for communicating with the microprocessor

Printer

Receives bytes from memory for printing characters and graphics

CD-RW

Removable storage for programs, data files, pictures, songs. Referred to as a "burner" because of the laser beam recording.

Flash Disk

Replacement for floppy disks. Removable storage for saving programs, data files, pictures, songs. Large electronic capacity, small size, rugged.

Maintaining Your Computer

Parts of a Window

When any program is opened (started), then it is referred to as an open window. They have a somewhat consistent appearance to them. The diagram below shows the My Computer program opened and "restored down" from the maximized view so that the Windows desktop can be identified as well.

Parts of a Window

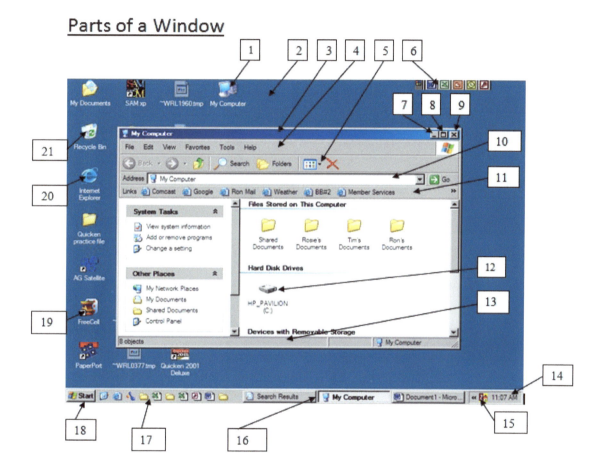

1. My Computer icon
2. Desktop
3. My Computer Title bar
4. Menu bar
5. Standard buttons toolbar
6. Office toolbar
7. Minimize button
8. Maximize button
9. Close button
10. Address window
11. Links toolbar
12. Hard drive icon
13. My Computer Status bar
14. Clock
15. Tray/Notification area
16. Task bar
17. Quick launch toolbar
18. Start button
19. Desktop Shortcut
20. IE icon
21. Recycle bin icon

Show Icons on Desktop (XP)

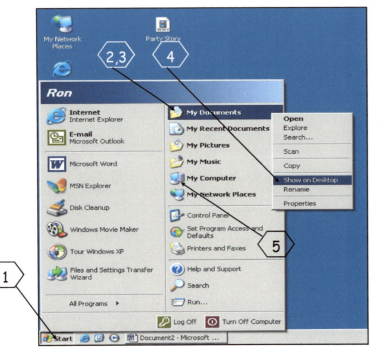

<u>Show icons for My Documents & My Computer on desktop</u>

This task should be done as a first step for using this book since the remainder of the book references these icons on the desktop instead of the Start Menu.

1. Click Start
2. Point to My Documents
3. Right click My Documents
4. Click Show on Desktop
5. Repeat for My Computer

Show icons on desktop for Documents & Computer

Note: "Documents" in Windows Vista is the "My Documents" in Windows XP, and "Computer" is "My Computer" in XP.

This task should be done as a first step for using this book since the remainder of the book references these icons on the desktop instead of the Start Menu. Understand that Documents in Vista equates to My Documents in XP, and Computer equates to My Computer.

1. Click Start

2. Point to Documents

3. Right drag "Documents" slightly to the right until a Documents icon appears on the desktop.

4. Click Create Shortcuts Here

5. Observe the Documents shortcut on the desktop. Drag it to a preferred location.

6. Repeat for "Computer"

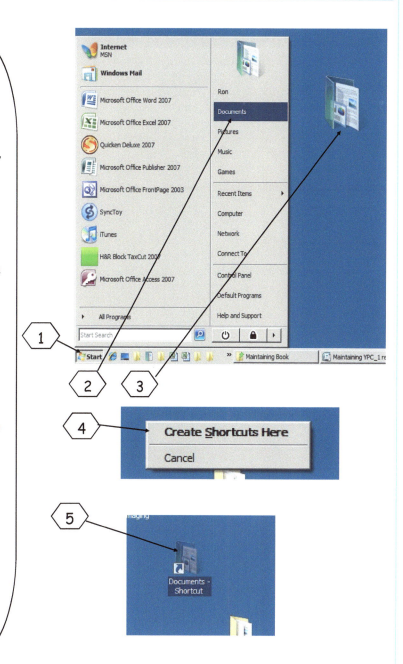

Checking System Resources

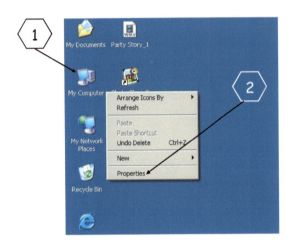

Checking System Resources
1. Right click My Computer
2. Click Properties
3. Click the General tab
4. Note the version of Windows, type of Processor, Clock speed (Hz value), the amount of RAM (memory).

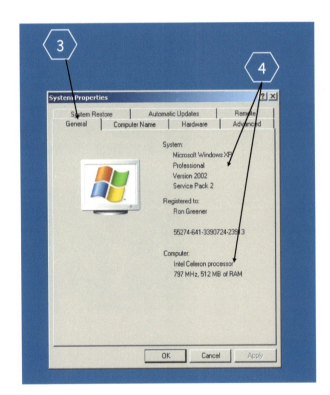

Checking Hard Disk Usage

1. Double-click My Computer.
2. Right-click Local Disk (C:).
3. Click Properties.
4. Note the bytes of Used, Free, and Capacity.

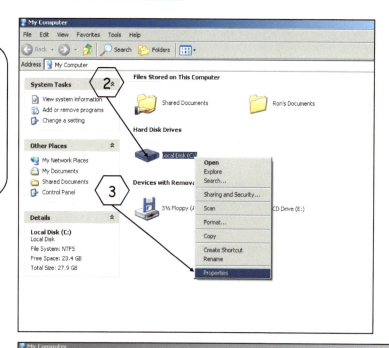

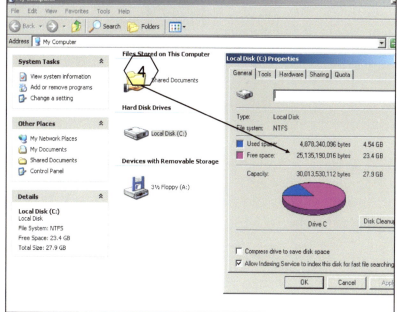

Disk Cleanup

Disk Cleanup is a Windows maintenance utility that provides for the removing of unneeded files that have built up on your hard disk. Running this task frees up hard disk space and provides the potential for improving overall performance. Run this once per month and preferably prior to doing a defragment.

Performing a Disk Cleanup

1. Perform the steps in "Hard Disk Usage" (pg. 9) to get the Local Disk Properties window.
2. Click the Disk Cleanup button
3. Observe the "calculating"
4. Check the 4 items shown (these 4 have always been good choices, the others are done at your discretion).
5. Click OK, then Yes, and observe the progress of the cleaning.

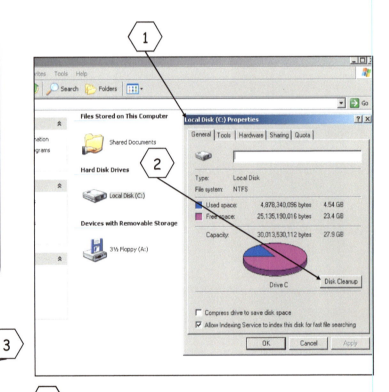

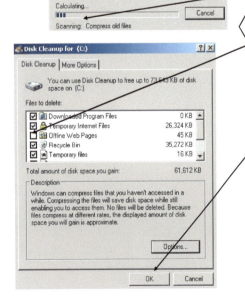

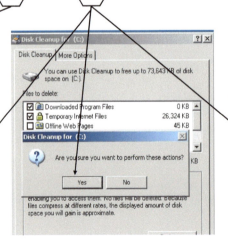

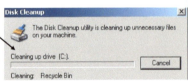

Check Disk (Chkdsk)

Check Disk (Chkdsk) checks the overall condition of the Hard Disk. Since the hard Disk is a mechanical device, it is more subject to failure than other parts of the computer. Check Disk checks for physical failure pertaining to the motors and read heads as well as software failure pertaining to corrupted files. Failure of either type, it attempts to correct. Run this at six month intervals or sooner should your computer be more than 2 years old.

To Run the Check Disk Program

1. Perform the steps in "Hard Disk Usage" (pg.9) to get the Local Disk Properties window.

2. Click the Tools tab.

3. Click the Check Now button

4. Click check-marks into both Check Disk options.

5. Click Start

6. Note the message that Check Disk cannot run when Windows is running.

7. Click Yes and Restart your computer.

8. Check Disk will start running as the boot cycle starts back up.

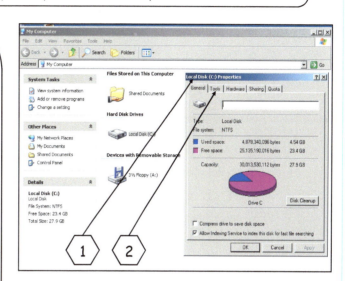

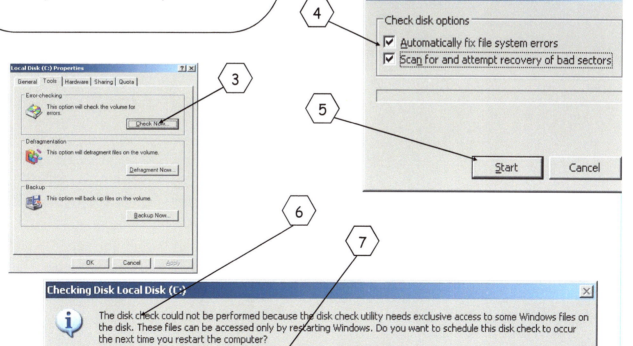

Defragmenting the Hard Disk

Fragmentation of files on the hard disk occurs as a result of Windows deleting files and then adding other files back in. The added files are stored in pieces according to the size of the deleted areas. A disk read command is required for each piece as opposed to just one read if the file were contiguous. Defragging puts the pieces together so as to improve system performance. This should be done once per month. Disk Cleanup & Check Disk should be done prior to the Defragmenting.

1. See Page 9 to open this window.
2. Click the Tools tab.
3. Click the Defragment Now button
4. Click the Analyze button
5. Check the results of the analysis to determine the need to defrag.
6. Click the Defragment button.
7. Observe the Defrag progress.
8. <u>NOTE</u>: For Windows Vista & 7, click the Start button, All Programs, Accessories, System Tools, Disk Defrag.

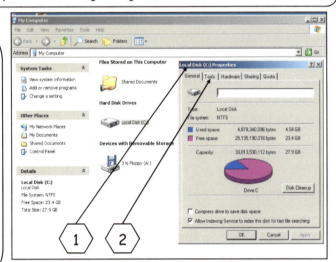

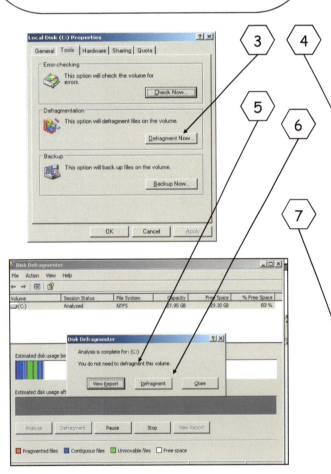

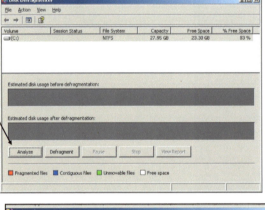

Maintaining Your Computer

Clearing Cache, Cookies, History Files

Clearing Cache, Cookies, History files

While browsing the Internet, your computer uses cache and history files to store specific information about a Web page on your hard drive. These files enable the browser to find the same pages more quickly when you access them later.

The cache file stores page information for quick retrieval; a cached page is accessed more easily than the original page; frequent updates by the browser ensure you are getting the most recent version.

The history file stores a running list of the sites you have visited in a given time period. Please remember each time you access a new page, new information is added to your hard drive that uses valuable space. Therefore, the cache and history files should be cleared on a regular basis--daily, if you visit a number of pages. Allowing information to accumulate in these files will slow your download speed.

If a web page is not displaying properly, or is displaying content that you believe is not current, the solution in most instances is to clear your Internet Explorer cache and cookie files.

Clearing Cache, Cookies, History files

1. Open the Internet Explorer window.
2. Click Tools from the menu bar (note: if the Menu Bar is not showing, go to the right side of the open window, click Tools, click Menu Bar)
3. Click Internet Options.
4. Click Delete
5. Click the Delete Files, then the Delete Cookies, and finally, Delete History.
6. Click Close.
7. Click OK.

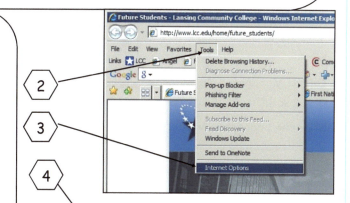

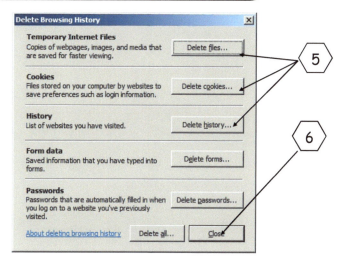

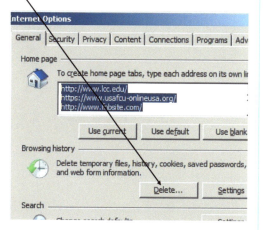

Maintaining Your Computer

Recovering from a Lockup

A computer that is locked up is one in which the user has lost the control of performing tasks such as clicking the mouse, typing text into a letter, or reading email. A deeper meaning to a lockup is that one of the programs running on the computer is in a program loop and therefore is "not responding" to the Windows master control program. The Windows XP operating system program provides a feature that allows for ending the "not responding" program so that the user can continue with performing tasks and therefore overcome the necessity to engage the Power Off pushbutton which one should take every measure to avoid so as to prevent file corruption.

When a lockup occurs:

1. With 2 fingers on your left hand, hold down the ALT and CTRL keys in the lower left of the keyboard.

2. Tap the DELETE key that is directly above the arrow keys.

3. Click Start Task Manager (Vista only)

4. On the Windows Task Manager window, click the Applications tab.

5. Click the program whose status is "Not Responding"

6. Click the End Task button.

7. Save any files that require saving.

8. Restart your computer

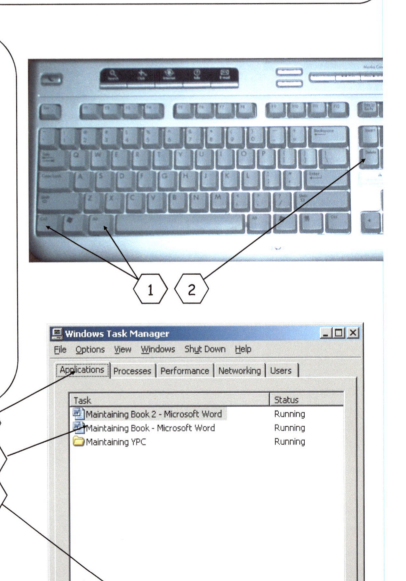

Maintaining Your Computer

Proper Shutdown of Your Computer

It is very important that your computer be shutdown properly. The reason behind the importance is that Windows has opened many files from the Hard Disk and transferred copies of them into the computer's memory. Prior to shutting down power, Windows needs to close those files plus do some additional housekeeping tasks. Should it not get the opportunity to do so, then when your computer is started back up, Windows is very confused by the condition of those files and finds it necessary to fix them before running your computer. Sometimes this is a rather insignificant problem and easily corrected by Windows. But depending on the situation, it can be a serious problem. In that case Windows runs special software like Checkdisk in an attempt to correct the problem. Another big reason to cycle down using the Shut Down command, is that some updates that have been downloaded from Microsoft, require that they be installed during the Shut Down cycle. So bottom line, does a lot of housekeeping that is a very healthy experience for your computer.

To Shut Down:

1. Click the Start button

2. Click Turn Off Computer (Vista, the black arrow)

3. Click Turn Off (Vista, Shut Down)

4. Allow the computer to cycle down and turn off power automatically

5. _Note_ that this procedure can be used to Re-start (reboot) which means loading a fresh copy of Windows into the computer's memory. This causes the computer to go through the same cycle down as Shut Down except that it does not power off, but instead, cycles back up.

6. _Note_ that Stand By does _not_ cause the cycle down to occur, but just puts the computer into a reduced power state.

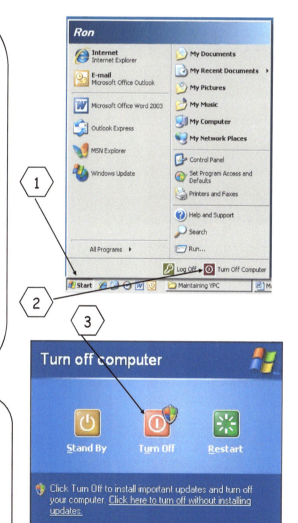

Is it OK to leave my computer on all of the time?

Answer: NO

The power down cycle provides:
1. Housekeeping
2. Installation of updates
3. Closes the door on hackers
4. Less prone to corruption due to power surges

Power Surge and Heat Protection

The technology used today (integrated circuits) in creating the electronic components within the computer, is rather amazing especially if you understand the migration from vacuum tubes to today's state of the art components. We the consumer, have benefitted immensely since we over time, have received more and more for less and less. Functionality has gone up, and cost has come down. For the most part, hardware failures are minimal. However, this technology is very sensitive to voltage surges and excessive heat. Measures must be taken to protect against these 2 environmental problems. Power strips that provide surge protection should be installed so as to prevent power line surges from entering into your computer. Regarding heat, your computer has built-in fans that exhaust the heated air out of the rear of the computer (side of a laptop). Check for airflow periodically.

Surge Protection Requirements:

1. Protection and Ground Indicators
2. Power connectors
3. On/off switch
4. Coax cable connectors
5. Phone line connectors
6. Ethernet cable connectors
7. Rated minimum *3000 joules*

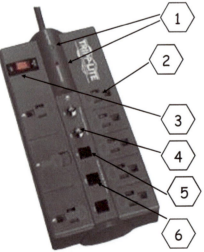

Checking the Cooling Fans

With your hand, check for airflow coming out from the fan grilles in the rear.

Tape a strip of tissue so that it hangs down and over the exhaust grille so as to detect airflow.

Look for air intake grilles along the sides, front or bottom. They can become clogged with dust thus restricting airflow.

Some computers have airflow detectors and/or overheat detectors that will prevent power from being applied in the case of fan failure or overheating.

You can remove the outer cover and check for accumulated dust within. In this case, be careful not to touch any of the electronics since they can be damaged by the static electricity buildup on your body. **Use only compressed air that has been purchased from a computer store to blow out the dust**

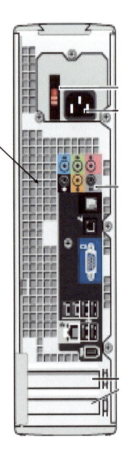

Battery Backup

Battery Backup Protection for Home Computers (UPS)

Another option for protecting your computer from power surges, is the Uninterrupted Power System (UPS) that provides battery backup power allowing you to work through short and medium length power outages. It also safeguards your equipment from damaging surges and spikes that travel along your utility and phone lines. (Coax cable surge protection is also included on selected models.) Software that comes with a UPS and is installed on your computer, will automatically shut down your computer system in the event of an extended power outage. These devices typically cost around $20 more than the power strip. The additional cost can be easily recovered in avoiding time lost in redoing lost files as well as preventing damage to the electronics because of power surges.

Maintaining Your Computer

Saving Electricity

Two devices, the display and the hard disk, account for using most of the overall power required by a computer. In periods of inactivity, such as when one is gone for lunch or a meeting, power to these devices can be made to shut-down without affecting the operation of the processor and memory which still have power and therefore continue to run. Following the shut-down, any activity such as moving the mouse, will cause a restoration of power and the computer commences running as it was at the point of shut-down.

Adjusting Power Shut-Down Delays

1. Minimize all open windows.
2. Click Start, Control Panel
3. Click Power Options
4. Click the Power Schemes tab.
5. Adjust the turn-off delays, meaning the time of no activity that prompts a power shut-down to that device.
6. Note: System Standby consists of shutting down the monitor, hard disk, and a reduction in power to the motherboard electronics.
7. Hibernate is a total power-off but a special one meaning that it saves the state that the computer is in at the time of shut-down. Hitting the Power-on button is required to restore the operation to the status at the point of shut-down.
8. For **Vista**, following step 3 above, **Energy Star** is recommended. For **Windows 7**, **Balanced Power Plan**

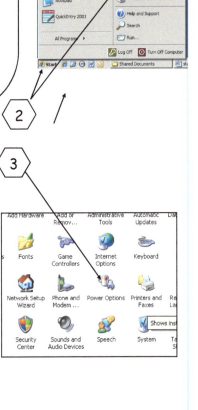

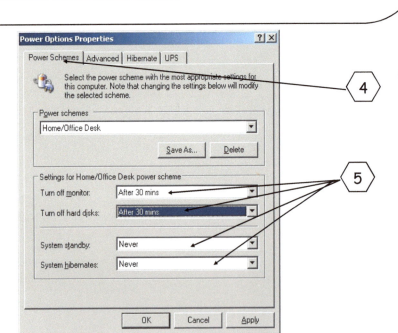

Purchasing the Correct Memory Module

The technology for manufacturing memory has made many changes over time. Therefore, there are many choices to choose from. Finding the correct part to install in your computer is best done with the help of an expert. Thus, the recommendation is to open the webpage www.4allmemory.com Here you can allow the website to access your computer and determine the type required. In addition, it also indicates the number of available slots, maximum capacity, modules currently installed, and a recommendation for adding more. You can then make a purchase thru that website or take the ordering information to a local dealer.

Purchasing Memory (RAM)

1. Open the website www.4allmemory.com

2. Click Check My System.

3. Click on the yellow bar and click Install ActiveX Control

4. Click Install again.

5. When the installation has completed, the website will then report the information pertinent to your PC

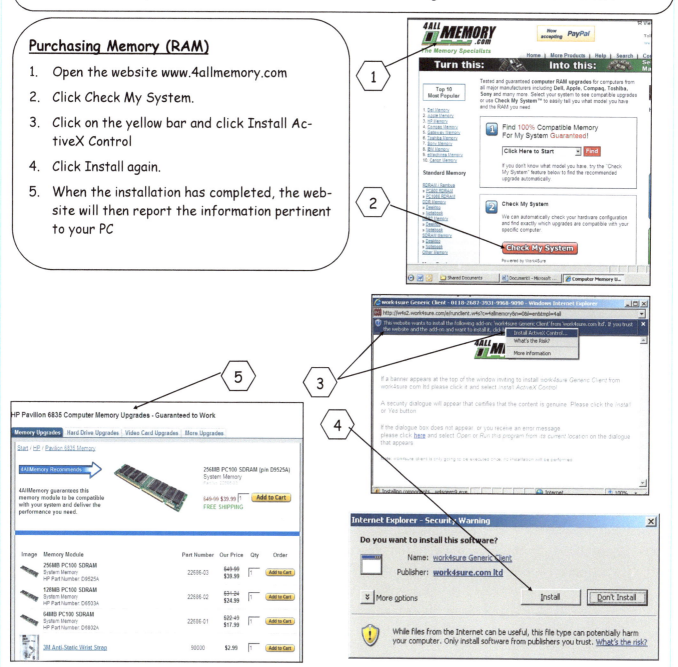

Memory (RAM) Installation

These instructions are general for most desktop PCs. Refer to your users manual for instructions specific to your PC. Some computers do require installing matched pairs or using specific slots. Gaining access to the memory sockets on a laptop, will usually be thru a panel that can be removed on the bottom.

Note: Before touching electronic components, make sure you are properly grounded. By wearing a wrist strap, you can prevent static electricity stored on your person from damaging an electronic component. Anti-static straps are available for purchase from electronic sales outlets or from 4allmemory.com.

1. The first thing to do is make sure the computer is shut down.

2. Note that it may seem sensible to unplug the computer before installing the memory, but keeping the machine plugged in will ground it, and this is important because that way any static electricity built up in your body will be discharged before handling the RAM chips. You can do this by touching any metal part of the case.

3. Remove the computer's cover following the instructions in your owner's manual.

4. Locate the memory expansion sockets on the computer's motherboard. If all the sockets are full, remove smaller capacity modules to allow room for higher capacity modules.

5. Once you've discharged your static electricity, pick up the memory chip by its top or sides. Don't touch the silver or gold contacts at the bottom, because even a little oil from your finger can eventually interfere with the connection. Regardless of the type of memory you have, it will only go into the empty memory slot one way, so look at the notches in the contacts and line them up so the partitions in the RAM sockets fit in the grooves.

6. Insert the module into an available expansion socket. Press the module into position, making certain the module is completely seated in the socket. The ejector tabs at each end of the socket will automatically snap into the locked position. Repeat this procedure for any additional modules you are installing. The ejector tabs shown in the illustration are used to remove a module. By pushing outward on the ejector tabs, the module will pop-up from the socket and it can then be removed.

Windows Update

Windows Update

Windows Update refers to downloading and installing the Security Vulnerability Patches that have been developed by Microsoft. These patches are modifications to the Windows program. A great deal of emphasis should be placed on the importance of making sure that your computer has these installed since they deal mainly with protecting your computer from being corrupted by unauthorized users (hackers). The procedure outlined below shows that your computer should be set to automatically download and install updates daily. This is done in the background without your consent which is a good thing.

1. Close all programs.

2. Click the Start button, point to Programs, then click Windows Update.

3. Click Change Settings

4. Verify that your settings are as shown below.

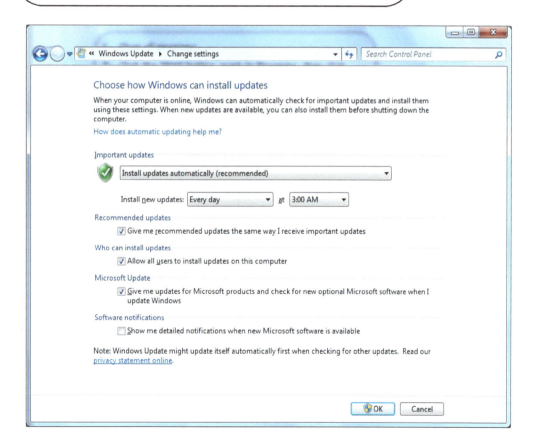

Maintaining Your Computer

Adding Program Shortcuts to the Desktop

Adding shortcuts to the desktop is done for the purpose of saving time. When we have a program that we use frequently, it might take a few mouse clicks in the programs start menu in order to open it up. Adding a shortcut to the desktop reduces the number of clicks to just one. Note that shortcuts are pointers to the actual program. Deleting them does no harm to the program.

This procedure shows adding a shortcut for the program Calculator.

1. Close all open windows.

2. Click START, ALL PROGRAMS, ACCESSORIES.

3. Point to the Calculator icon and **right** drag it to the a blank area on the desktop.

4. Click Create Shortcut Here.

5. <u>CAUTION: BE CERTAIN NOT TO CLICK MOVE WHICH WOULD CAUSE THE ICON TO BE REMOVED FROM THE START MENU</u>

This topic is meant to explain how you, the user, should be saving files on your computer. First it is important to understand that the files that we are referring to here, are, for example, letters that we write to a customer, or invoices, or spreadsheets created with Excel, pictures from our camera, music ripped from a CD. In other words, user created files.

Saving means that files are first placed into the computer's memory and then must be transferred (saved) onto the computer's hard disk. For example, as we type a letter, the typing is being entered into the memory, a temporary storage area which is totally erased when power is shut down. So in the event that power to your computer is lost or the computer locks-up and has to be restarted, typing that was not saved to the hard disk (permanent storage), is therefore lost and must be re-done.

Saving user files on a computer is analogous to saving files in a file cabinet with folders and papers within folders. In the computer, the file cabinet is the My Documents folder that we typically find on the computer's desktop. Then within the My Documents, we create sub-folders just as we would hang folders into a file cabinet. Then within the sub-folders, we save our files just like we put papers into the file cabinet folders.

It is important that this be understood and followed so that when a backup of the My Documents is performed, all of the user files are backed-up. Sometimes when user programs are purchased such as personal finance or tax programs, the saving location is other than the My Documents folder. In this case, refer to the programs preferences for the saving location so that you can either change it or make certain that it is backed-up separately from the My Documents backup.

Saving Files

1. Open MS Word.
2. Type a letter.
3. Click File.
4. Point to Save As
5. Type a file name
6. Click My Documents
7. Click New Folder
8. Type a folder name
9. Click OK
10. Click Save
11. Close out of Word
12. Open My Documents
13. Double-click the sub-folder
14. Double-click the file icon to open the file

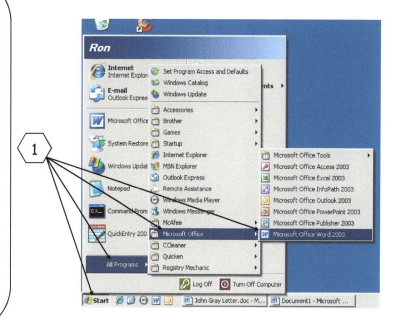

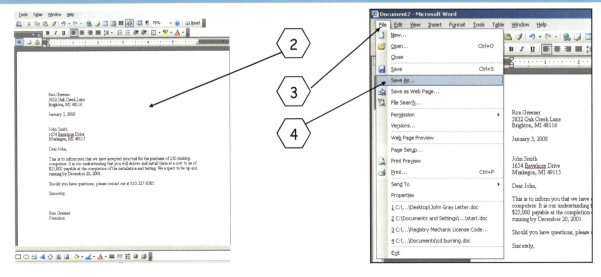

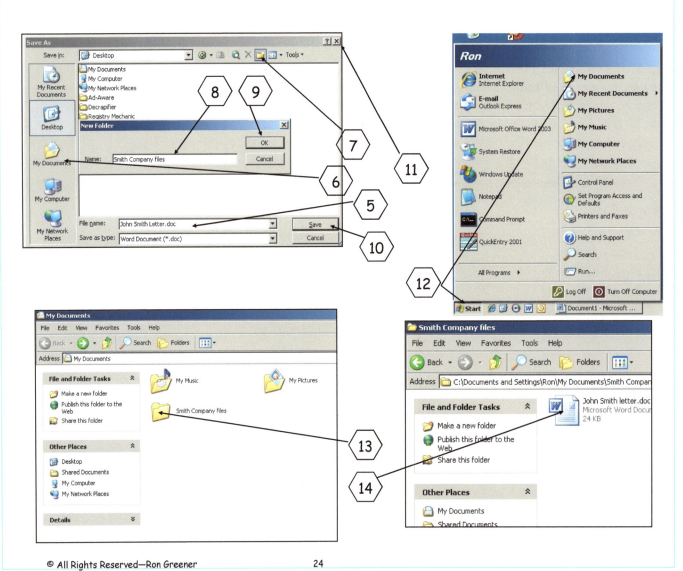

Maintaining Your Computer

Renaming Files and Folders

Renaming Files and Folders

Occasionally names given to files or folders have a need to be changed so as to be more meaningful. Pictures that are downloaded from your camera are a good example of this since they are given an almost meaningless name by the camera. For this example we will use the folder and file created in the procedure "How and Where to Save Files".

Renaming files and Folders

1. Open the My Documents folder

2. Right-click the "Smith Company files" folder

3. Click Rename

4. Tap the Delete key

5. Type a new name for the folder

6. Tap the Enter key

7. Double-click the folder to open it

8. Repeat the procedure for the "John Smith letter.doc" file.

9. Note that when the 3 character extension (doc) is showing, that should remain unchanged in the process of renaming.

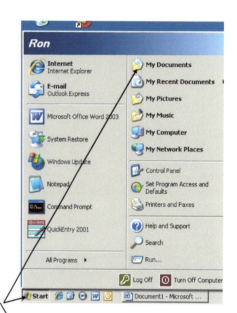

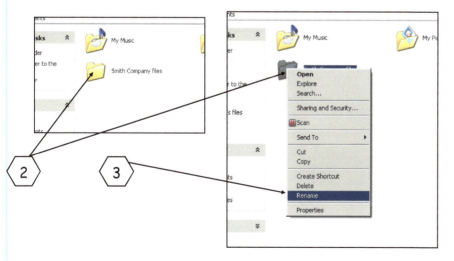

File Management

Documents that we create on the computer are called user files. These files are normally kept in sub-folders that are in the Documents folder. If you have been doing this correctly over time, then the Documents folder should be 100% yellow icons (folders). Non-yellow items (files) are meant to be placed inside of the yellow folders. This is the same analogy that is used with a file cabinet where the file cabinet is the Documents folder, the Pandaflex folders are the computer's sub-folders, and the paper documents are the files on the computer. The right mouse is a good choice for making folders (rt-click, new, folder) and then cutting & pasting or copying & pasting the files into folders.

Customer files all mixed together, not organized into sub-folders.

Folders made with the right mouse.

Files are then Cut & Pasted into the folders.

Maintaining Your Computer

Finding Lost Files

Finding files that you know that you saved on the hard disk, but when you come back to open them, you find that they did not save as you thought they did. This can be frustrating. Starting with Windows Vista and the Windows 7, we are provided with an excellent Search and Find feature.

1. Click on the Start Button in the lower left corner of the desktop.

2. Begin entering the name of the file or folder that you trying to locate.

3. As you type, suggested file/folder names begin to appear. This list changes as you continue to type.

4. Once you see the file/folder, you have choices. Click on it to open it up. Or, right click and select Open File Location.

5. Once you open the location and verify that it got saved incorrectly, you can then cut and paste the file/folder to the Documents folder

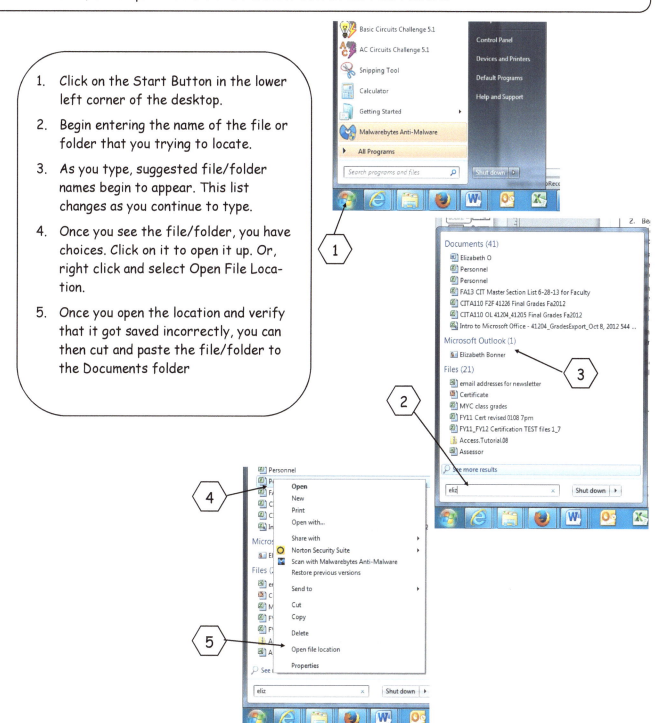

Saving Files/Folders to a Flash Disk

Flash Disk, sometimes referred to as Thumb Drive, is an increasingly popular external disk drive. It connects to the computer through any USB port and therefore is said to be a removable device that can be used for transferring files from one computer to another. It can also be used as a backup device for saving a copy of your personal files/folders. They can be purchased in sizes of 2, 4, 8, or 16GB (16 gigabytes or 16,000,000,000 bytes) and at a very reasonable cost. They have replaced the 1.44MB floppy disk (one 2GB flash equals 1400 floppy disks). They are easy to use, store and are very reliable. They require no formatting prior to use and are totally erasable and therefore are preferred over the CD-RW disk for saving data files. They are easily forgotten when used on other than your everyday computer. Thus labeling them electronically with your name is a wise idea (see pg. 25)

Saving Files/Folders to a Flash Disk

1. Plug the Flash Disk into any USB port.

2. Wait for the Flash Disk window to appear. Note the drive letter. Close that window.

3. Open the My Documents folder.

4. Right-click the folder or file of interest.

5. Click Send To

6. Click the drive letter from step #2 (this saves a **copy** to the Flash)

7. Refer to the procedure "Using My Computer" to verify that the files/folder are stored on the Flask Disk.

8. Note: **Flash Disks should be renamed** to YOUR-NAME so that they are easily identified. Do so by opening My Computer, right-click the flash disk icon, click Rename, type your name, Enter.

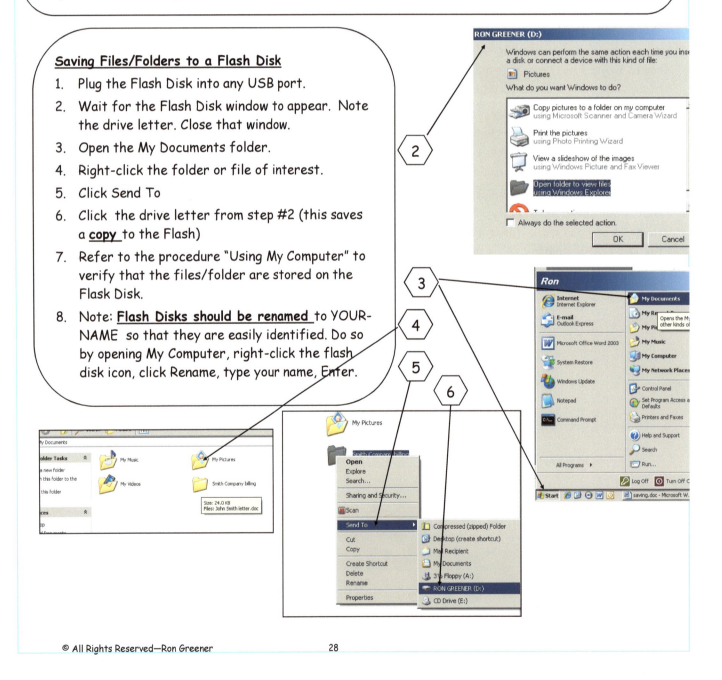

Maintaining Your Computer

Using the My Computer Program

Using My Computer

My Computer is a program that is used for displaying the contents of disk drives. It could be a case where you have just saved a file or folder to your removable Flash Disk so that you can transfer it to your work computer. You want to verify that the file is really saved there. Or maybe you've just done a backup of the My Documents folder and you want to verify that an exact copy of the My Documents has been saved on your External Hard Disk.

This procedure is demon-strated by using a Flash Disk. However, it could be the Hard Disk (C:), or the CD disk as well.

1. Insert a Flash Disk into any USB port.

2. Close out of any windows that popup.

3. Click the Start button

4. Click My Computer

5. Double-click the removable device icon that represents your Flash Disk.

6. The window that opens shows the contents of the Flash Disk.

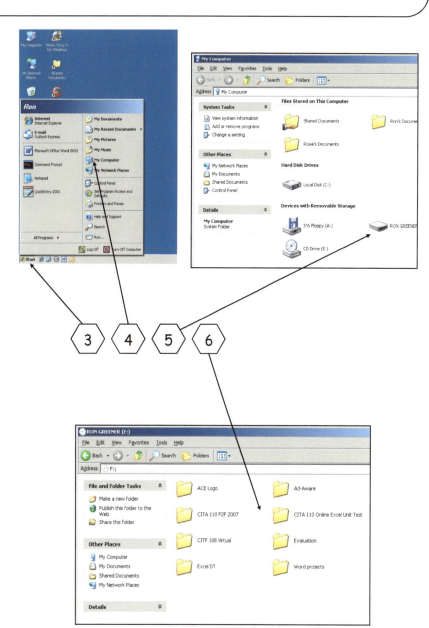

Safely Remove a Flash Disk or External Hard Disk

Safe Removal of Flash Disk or External Hard Disk

Proper removal is required in order to prevent loss of data.

1. Minimize all open windows so that the desktop is the only item displayed.

2. In the lower, right-hand corner, locate the green arrow icon that suggests removal of a device.

3. Pointing to it should display "Safely Remove Hardware".

4. Single, left-click it so as to produce the strip "Safely remove USB Mass Storage Device Drive X" or "Eject Flash Disk"

5. Left-click the strip. Or Eject Flash Disk" When "Safe to Remove Hardware" appears, remove the USB device

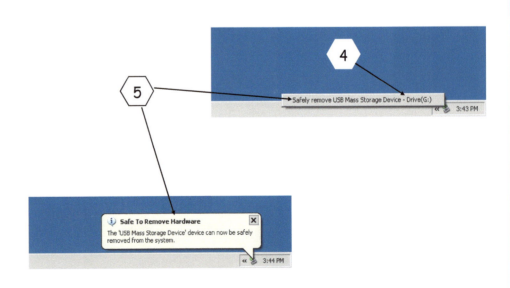

Labeling a Flash Disk or External Hard Disk

Labeling your Flash Disk or External Hard Disk means to put an electronic label on it that is seen whenever the icon for that device appears in a window. Doing this provides a couple of advantages.. First, it can be easily identified when viewed in a window where it is mixed in with other devices. Secondly, when used in a public computer such as a library or school, removal is sometimes forgotten. Labeling it with your name provides a better chance of claiming it.

Labeling a Flash Disk or External Hard Disk

1. Plug the disk unit into any USB port.

2. Close all windows .

3. Open the My Computer window.

4. Right-click the icon for the removable device

5. Click Rename

6. Enter a name (limited to 11 characters)

7. Hit the Enter key.

8. Safely remove the device (see procedure)

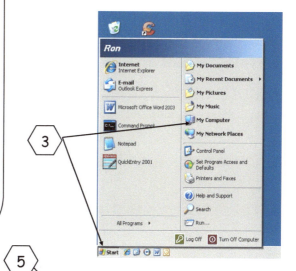

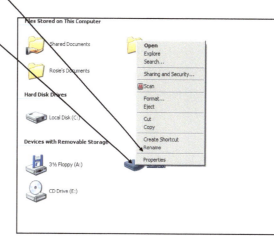

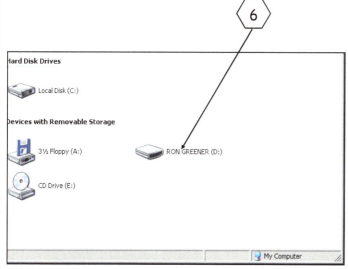

Maintaining Your Computer

Backing Up Your User Files Windows XP (pg 1 of 2)

Backing up your My Documents folder and files is a very important part of maintaining your computer. It should be understood that the My Documents folder is the only place where files are to be saved as you go about using your computer daily. This means letters that you have written, spreadsheets, databases, pictures from your camera, music that you have downloaded, income tax files, personal finance files, etc. Backing up means to save a copy of the contents to a removable device such as a external Hard Disk (recommend an 200GB size) or a Flash Disk (recommend an 32GB size). Then store the removable device in a safe place so as to prevent it from being stolen or damaged. Also, understand that when the My Documents folder is copied to the external device, then all of the files and folders within My Documents are copied as well.

Procedure for Backing Up User Files (see next page for picture)

1. Insert your backup device (Flash Disk or External Hard Disk) into any USB port. USB ports can be found on the front, side, or rear of your computer.

2. From the Windows desktop, right click the START button.

3. Click Explore to open the Windows Explorer.

4. In the left pane, find Documents and Settings.

5. Click the + symbol so as to expand the sub-folders within Documents and Settings.

6. Find the folder with your name and click it once. This causes the contents of that folder to be displayed in the right pane.

7. In the right pane, right-click the My Documents icon and then click Send To.

8. In the list that appears, click the backup device that you have plugged into the USB port. This causes a copy of My Documents to be saved on the backup device

9. Repeat step 6 and 7 for the Desktop folder and the Favorites folder.

10. Most users have just the one account set up on their computer. However, if you have individual accounts for other users, then repeat steps 1-9 for all other accounts.

11. Make a folder on the backup device (right-click on white space, click New, then folder).

12. Rename the folder (use right-click) to Backup MMDDYYYY where the M,D,Y are the current date.

13. Drag all of the backed-up folders onto the Backup MMDDYYYY

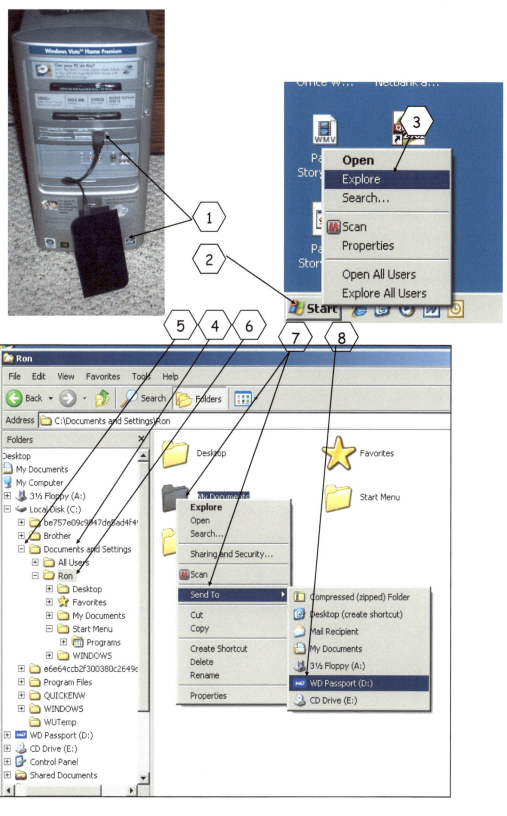

Backing Up Your User Files Windows Vista & 7

Backing up your user files is a very important part of maintaining your computer. This means letters that you have written, spreadsheets, databases, pictures from your camera, music that you have down-loaded, income tax files, personal finance files, etc. Backing up means to save a copy of the contents to a removable device such as a external Hard Disk (recommend an 200GB size) or a Flash Disk (recommend an 32GB size). Then store the removable device in a safe place so as to prevent it from being stolen or damaged.

Procedure for Backing Up User Files Windows Vista & Windows 7

1. Insert your backup device (Flash Disk or External Hard Disk) into any USB port. USB ports can be found on the front, side, or rear of your computer.

2. From the Windows desktop, click the START button.

3. Find your name in the upper right corner of the Start Menu. Click it.

4. Note that a "yourname" folder opens and displays all of your personal user files.

5. Hold down the CTRL key and click the following folders: CONTACTS, DESKTOP, FAVOR-ITES, LINKS, MY DOCUMENTS, MY MUSIC, MY PICTURES, MY VIDEOS. They should all be selected (highlighted).

6. Let up on the CTRL key. Then right-click anyone of the highlighted folders.

7. Point to SEND TO and then click on the icon for your flash disk. This causes all of the selected folders to be copied to your backup device.

8. Using MY COMPUTER, open the backup device and verify that the copy took place.

9. Make a folder on the backup device (right-click on white space, click New, then folder).

10. Rename the folder (use right-click) to Backup MMDDYYYY where the M,D,Y are the current date.

11. Drag all of the backed-up folders onto the Backup MMDDYYYY

12. Most users have just the one account set up on their computer. However, if you have individual accounts for other users, then repeat steps 1-11 for all other accounts.

Maintaining Your Computer

Spyware Protection

Spyware is software that can install itself and run on your computer without providing you with adequate notice, consent, or control. Spyware might not display symptoms after it infects your computer, but can affect how your computer runs. Spyware can, for example, monitor your online behavior or collect information about you (including personally identifiable or other sensitive information) and sell it to advertisers. It can change settings on your computer. It can be a major cause of your computer running slow.

Spyware can be best prevented by keeping an up to date anti-spyware program running on your computer. When you purchase protection for your computer, be certain to select an "Internet Security" package which includes anti-virus, anti-spyware, and a firewall. PC-Cillin is recommended due to experience, but Norton and McAfee are also well recognized products.

Note that *PC-Cillin Internet Security* is running on this computer. The presence of the PC-Cillin capsule in the lower right corner of your desktop, indicates that it is running in the background all of the time. Double-click to open the information panel shown below. The date shown in "Last Update" indicates when the most current definition files have been downloaded from the provider. These programs are written so that they will do automatic updates. Therefore, that date should be checked periodically for being not more than 2 days old. This ensures that your subscription (typically 1 year) is still valid and the protection is current.

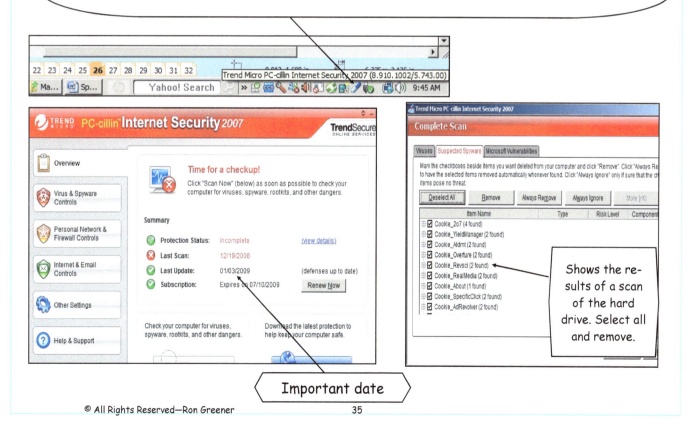

Shows the results of a scan of the hard drive. Select all and remove.

Important date

Anti-Virus Protection

Computer viruses are programs written by highly skilled individuals who are seeking fame and bragging rights. Viruses find their way into your computer through the Internet meaning email, and the downloading of webpage content. Once into your computer, they spread, use valuable resources, cause your computer to run slow, and in some cases do damage to the point of requiring total recovery of the hard disk. Obviously it is extremely important to have an anti-virus program installed, up to date, and always running in the background.

When you purchase protection for your computer, be certain to select an "Internet Security" package which includes anti-virus, anti-spyware, and a firewall. PC-Cillin is recommended due to experience, but Norton and McAfee are also well recognized products.

Note that *PC-Cillin Internet Security* is running on this computer. The presence of the PC-Cillin capsule in the lower right corner of your desktop, indicates that it is running in the background all of the time. Double-click to open the information panel shown below. The date shown in "Last Update" indicates when the most current definition files have been downloaded from the provider. These programs are written so that they will do automatic updates. Therefore, that date should be checked periodically for being not more than 2 days old. This ensures that your subscription (typically 1 year) is still valid and the protection is current.

Important date

Steps to Virus Protection

1. Install the latest Microsoft updates
2. Purchase a reputable antivirus program
3. After purchasing an antivirus program, scan your entire computer to be sure it is free of malware
4. Update your antivirus definitions regularly
5. Be suspicious of any and all unsolicited e-mail attachments
6. Stay informed about viruses and virus hoaxes
7. Install a personal firewall program
8. Download software only if you are sure the Web site is legitimate.
9. Avoid as best you can visiting unscrupulous Web sites

Maintaining Your Computer

Malwarebytes Spyware Cleaner

Having a good Internet Security Package installed on your computer is the first defense in preventing virus and spyware. Norton, McAfee, and PC-Cillin are examples. However, Malwarebytes is another good choice for scanning your hard disk when you suspect a virus. It is a free download from the Internet that only runs when you tell it to do so. Therefore it does not run in competition with your installed anti-virus program. This program seems to find virus when others do not. I suggest uninstalling it when you have finished your scan otherwise you might be pestered to buy the full version.

Installing and Running MalewareBytes
(Screenshots from Google Chrome Browser)

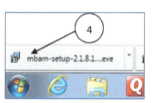

Click through the prompts to complete the installation and then it will automatically flow into running the MalwawreBytes program.

Maintaining Your Computer

Uninstalling a Program

There are many reasons why we may want to uninstall a program. One, it came installed from the factory and we just don't need it (games). Two, our current anti-virus program needs to be removed before we can install a recently purchased new one. Three, a webpage appeared indicating that our computer has problems and we made the mistake of allowing a "free scan" of our hard disk (Rogue Malware). Four, we downloaded a program from the Internet, tried it, and now want to remove it. CAUTION: Some of the installed programs listed are required for proper running of your computer. Be certain of what you are deleting.

Uninstalling a Program

1. Click the Start button.

2. Click Control Panel

3. Click Programs, Uninstall a program. Note your computer may be set to bypass this step. If so, then click on Programs and features to get the screen as shown for step #4.

4. Right click the program to be uninstalled

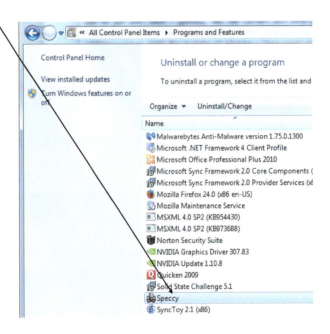

Installing the Firefox Browser

Internet Explorer is the choice of browser (a program designed to read webpage content) for most who read email and surf the web. Many think that this is what they have to use since it came with the Windows program. An equally good and most likely better browser, is the Mozilla Firefox browser which is a free download from the web. Firefox came about as a result of third party individuals who saw the flaws and inefficiency of Internet Explorer and decided to produce Firefox. It is maintained and updated by the Mozilla Corporation.

1. The following steps apply to using the IE browser.

2. Google "Firefox"

3. Select the link pointing to Download Mozilla Firefox

4. Click RUN

5. Click RUN when the setup.exe file appears.

6. Click YES to the User Account Control window.

7. Follow the prompts to install and run Firefox

Maintaining Your Computer

Creating a Restore Point

System Restore is a feature within Windows XP that allows for the rolling back of any changes to the Windows environment such as Registry Keys and installed programs so that in the event of a malfunction, the system can be set to a previous, working state. A manual restore point should be taken whenever the plan is to make a significant change to Windows and/or the installed programs. Note that user files saved during the period of roll-back, are not lost due to the roll-back.

Creating a Restore Point

1. Click Start, Programs, Accessories, System Tools, System Restore.

2. In the Welcome screen, click a radial dot into Create a Restore Point and Next.

3. Enter an appropriate description and click Create.

4. Observe the Restore Point Created window and Close

5. Install changes

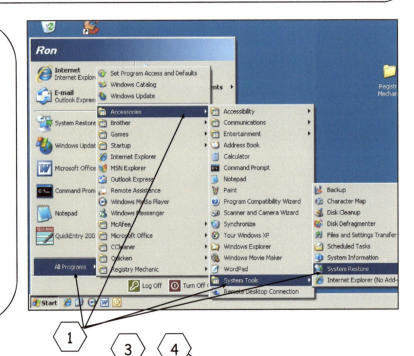

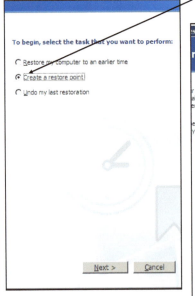

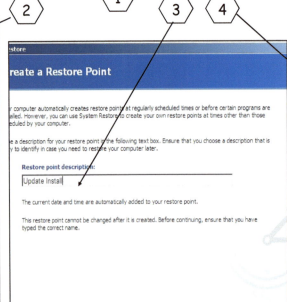

Restore Point Roll-Back

In the event of a malfunction of the system following a change to the Windows environment, a roll-back to a previously created Restore Point can be accomplished. This will return the Registry settings to those saved in the restore point and remove any programs installed following the taking of the Restore Point.

Rolling Back to a Previously Created Restore Point

1. Click Start, Programs, Accessories, System Tools, System Restore.

2. Click a radial dot into Restore My Computer to an Earlier Time. And next.

3. In the next screen, select the restore point of choice and next.

4. Then Confirm and next.

5. Observe that Windows will restart and in the process, roll-back the Registry and installed programs.

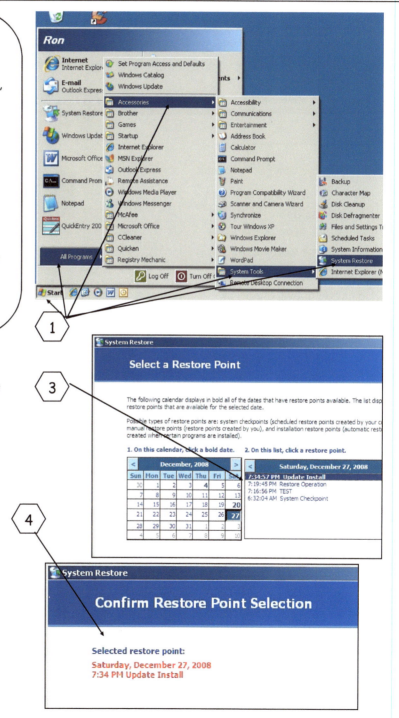

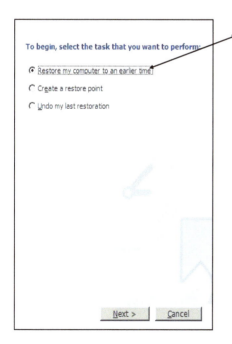

Monitoring System Performance

Windows XP has a program within the Task Manager for monitoring the load on the microprocessor (CPU). It displays CPU Usage as a percent of its maximum ability. So if the usage shows 25% then the processor is running at 25% of its maximum ability. This is especially useful when you first turn on your computer because it is very busy at that time. Allowing it to settle down to a normal 2-4%, will prevent a lot of mouse clicking for which poor or no response is seen. This can cause confusion to you the user as well as to Windows.

Monitoring System Performance

1. With 2 fingers on your left hand, hold down the ALT and CTRL keys in the lower left of the keyboard.

2. Tap the DELETE key that is directly above the arrow keys.

3. On the Windows Task Manager window, click the Performance tab.

4. After the computer has had sufficient time to boot-up, CPU usage should be in the 2-4% range.

5. Start a program like Word and notice the increased CPU activity.

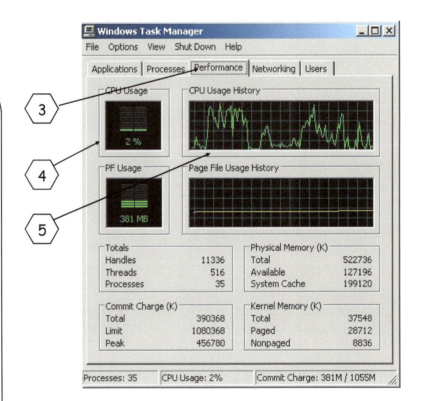

Screen Capture

Screen Capture is a feature of the Windows operating system wherein the image being displayed on the screen can be copied into the Windows clipboard. Following that you can then paste the contents of the clipboard into a word-processing document such as Word. This feature is useful when you have a need to communicate to another what the screen looks like for specific task. The example used to demonstrate this feature is capturing the system resources that are displayed in the System Properties window and then paste them into an MS Word document.

Screen Capture of the desktop

1. Refer to the Checking System Resources that is described in the front of this book (see Table of Contents).

2. With the screen shown below, tap the Print Scr key that is in the top row of the keyboard directly above the arrow keys. (or hold ALT & tap Print Scr for the active window only)

3. Open a blank Word document.

4. Click the paste button and note that the screen image then appears in the blank Word document.

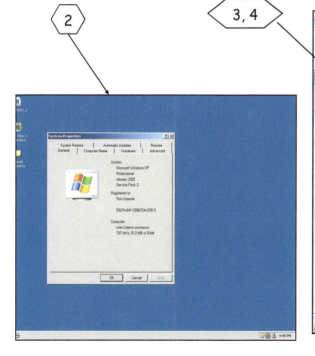

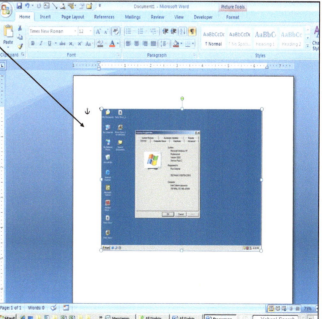

Maintaining Your Computer

Screen Resolution

Screen Resolution. Screen resolution refers to the number of dots (pixels) that appear on the screen (display). The most common screen resolution is 1024x768. This means that there are 1024 dots across (horizontal) by 768 dots down (vertical), a 4 to 3 ratio. Changing the resolution will cause the amount of screen content to change as well as the size of the content. For example, if the resolution is set to a higher setting, then more content is displayed but the content is smaller and could be harder to read. A lower setting nets in less content but larger items and thus easier to read.

Adjusting Screen resolution.

1. Right-click any empty area on the desktop.

2. Left-click Screen Resolution.

3. Left-drag the slider to the desired setting.

4. Click Apply and Ok.

5. In the process of making the change, the screen will go black for about 2 seconds.

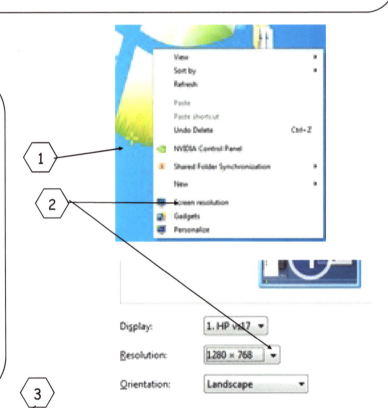

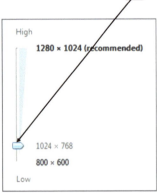

Adding Files to a Zip Folder for Emailing

Windows provides a feature called a ZIP folder. The best thing about it is that it is a folder but also a folder that looks like a file . And since it looks like a file, it can be attached to an email, something that a normal folder cannot. Placing files into the zip folder provides the ability to email several files all at once, something that otherwise either cannot be done or is time consuming to do. In addition, the files are compressed, meaning smaller size, which is a plus for emailing. Once removed from the folder, they return to their normal size and content.

Adding files to a zip folder for emailing.

1. Copy the files of interest to the computer desktop.

2. Right-click a vacant (blank) area of the desk-top.

3. Point to New, then over and down to Com-pressed (zipped) Folder, and left click it.

4. Type into the filename (or rt-clk & rename) making certain to include the .zip extension (for example, myassignments.zip).

5. Drag each of the files onto the top of the zip folder.

6. Double-click the zip folder to confirm that the files are within.

7. The zip folder with the files inside is now ready for attaching to an email.

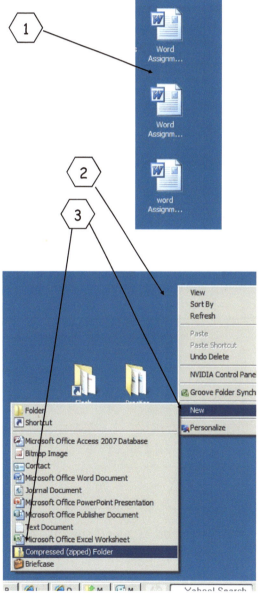

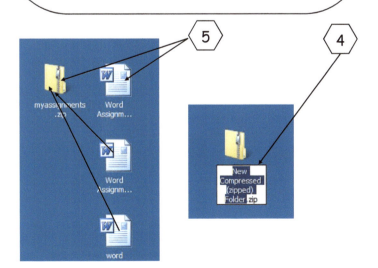

Line speed refers to the rate at which data is transferred into and out of your computer. This is good information to know because at times we are fooled into thinking that our computer is performing slowly when, in reality, it's the line speed that is slow thereby making us think that the computer has a performance problem. Line speed is measured in Mbps, or better said as Megabits per second. Dividing the Megabits per second by 8 provides the speed in Megabytes per second since there are 8 bits per byte. This test provides both an upload rate meaning the rate at which data is transferred from your computer to an Internet server and also, a download rate meaning the rate at which data is sent from an Internet server to your computer. The download speed is designed to be significantly higher than the upload speed because your computer receives data in large volumes when a web page is requested whereas the data required to request a webpage is very small. The line speed is controlled by your service provider.

Checking Your Line Speed

1. **Open the Internet Explorer**
2. **Open the website** www.speakeasy.net
3. **Click the SPEED TEST button**
4. **Select a city to test from (Chicago in this case)**
5. **Take note of the reported numbers.**
6. **Contact your service provider for their opinion.**
7. **Measure a friends computer that has a somewhat equal service provider and compare.**

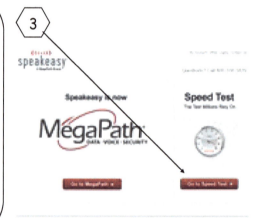

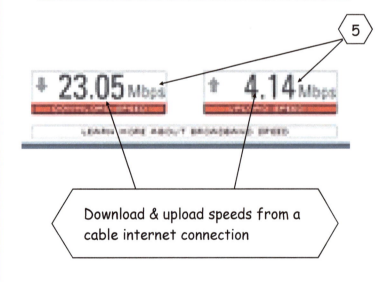

Download & upload speeds from a cable internet connection

46

Install a Router for Hacker Protection

If you have a cable or DSL connection, a home-networking router is recommended. This is a device that directs traffic between a single internet connection and one or more PCs on a local network. The router offers protection against several kinds of Internet-based attacks and provides an inexpensive and simple but effective layer of protection even if you have just one computer.

To connect to the Internet or any other network, a computer must have an IP (Internet Protocol) address. A hacker who learns this address (or chooses it at random) can try to invade your computer. Certain Internet worms like Sasser and Blaster make rapid-fire attacks on all possible IP addresses, looking for vulnerable computers.

When you have a router in place, your computer gets all the benefits of connecting to the Internet, without the risk of getting hacked via its IP address. The router accomplishes this through the magic of Network Address Translation. Each computer on the network receives a local-only IP address from the router, usually something like 192.168.x.x. This type of address is completely invisible outside the local network. Any hacker poking at the outward-facing IP address sees only the router.

It is recommended that you purchase a router with a built-in firewall that uses Stateful Packet Inspection which means that the firewall keeps a log of every outbound data packet and checks incoming packets against this log. Any incoming packet that doesn't match an outbound request is blocked.

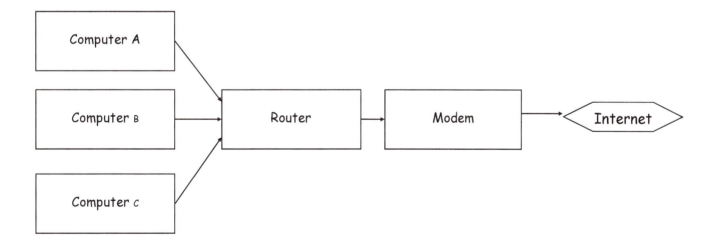

Maintaining Your Computer

Copy and Paste

Copy and paste is demonstrated here by taking text from an email and putting it into a Word document so that it can be printed or saved. The same can be applied to text or pictures within a webpage. This is a very practical thing to do since printing from an email or webpage is difficult to control. You may get more than needed, or a format that is not suitable.

> Emailed text that has been highlighted, then right-click over the top of the selected text, and left click copy

> Emailed text from above. Right-click into the Word document, then left-click paste.

Maintaining Your Computer

Adding an Attachment to an Email

Adding an attachment to an email means adding a file, such as a Word document or a picture. Most email programs show a paperclip as the symbol for attachment of a file. You click on the paperclip, then browse to the Documents or Pictures folder, arriving finally at the file of interest that when selected and then opened, will attach to the email for sending. The receiving party then sees the file name next to the paperclip, double-clicks the file name which then opens the file so that it can be read and likely saved to the Documents folder.

Adding an Attachment

1. Click the paperclip

2. Click Browse

3. Navigate to the file of interest

4. Click Open

5. Note that the filename is shown as attached.

6. Send the email

Receiving an attachment

1. Double-click the filename shown next to the paperclip

2. The file opens and then can be read, saved, printed.

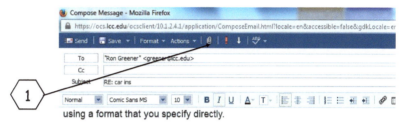

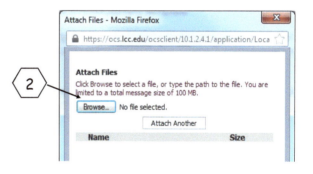

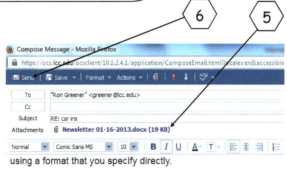

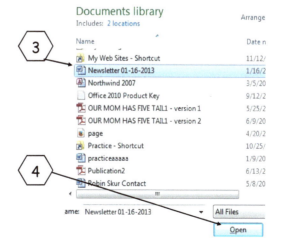

Windows ReadyBoost

Windows ReadyBoost is a feature provided by Windows Vista and Windows 7 that has the potential for improving the performance of your computer. It is easily installed. Uninstalling is likewise easily done just by removing the ReadyBoost flash disk.

1. Plug a flash drive (minimum 2 gigabyte) into any one of your computer's USB ports. This should automatically open an AutoPlay window.
2. If AutoPlay does not open, then open "Computer", right-click the Flash Drive, left-click Properties.
3. Under General Options, click Speed up my system.
4. This will display the Properties dialog box for your flash drive or other removable media device.
5. Click the ReadyBoost tab, and then do one of the following:
6. To turn ReadyBoost off, click Do not use this device.
7. To turn ReadyBoost on, click Use this device, and then move the slider to choose how much of the available space on your flash drive you want to reserve for boosting your system speed. The more the better but at least 2 GB.
8. Click OK.

Maintaining Your Computer

CCleaner

CCleaner (formerly **Crap Cleaner**), developed by Piriform, is a utility program used to clean potentially unwanted files (including temporary internet files, where malicious programs and code tend to reside) and invalid Windows Registryentries from a computer. CCleaner can delete temporary or potentially unwanted files left by certain programs, including Internet Explorer,Firefox, Google Chrome, Opera, Safari, Windows Media Player, eMule, Google Toolbar, Netscape, Microsoft Office,Nero, Adobe Acrobat, McAfee, Adobe Flash Player, Sun Java, WinRAR, WinAce, WinZip and GIMP [8] along with browsing history, cookies, recycle bin, memory dumps, file fragments, log files, system caches, application data,autocomplete form history, and various other data.[9] The program also includes a registry cleaner to locate and correct problems in the Windows registry, such as missing references to shared DLLs, unused registration entries for file extensions, and missing references to application paths. CNET editors gave the application a rating of 5/5 stars, calling it a 'must have tool'.

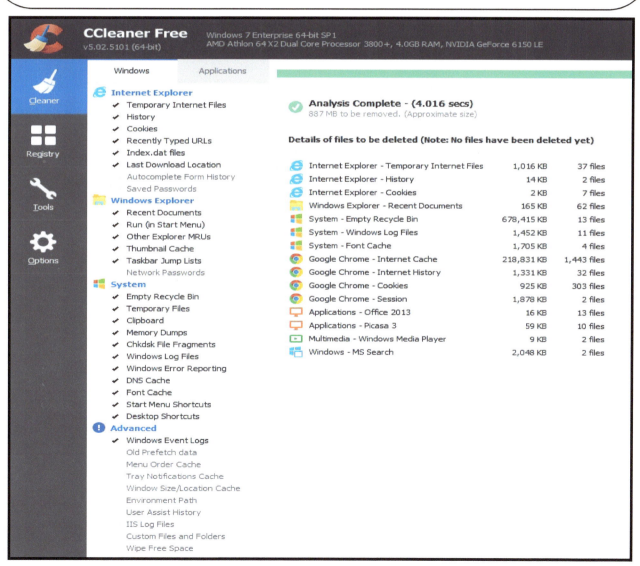

51